JOHN COOK'S
CIVIL WAR
STORY

KATIE MARSICO
ILLUSTRATED BY DAVID BELMONTE

Lerner Publications ◆ Minneapolis

PUBLISHER'S NOTE

This story is based on historical events. The people, places, and dates are known through primary source accounts of the time. While inspired by known facts, dialogue and some descriptive details have been fictionalized.

To my two sons—CJ and Thomas—like John, you are eager leaders, fearless fighters, and young men that are forever willing to help anyone in need. I am so proud of you!

Copyright © 2018 by Lerner Publishing Group, Inc.

All rights reserved. International copyright secured. No part of this book may be reproduced, stored in a retrieval system, or transmitted in any form or by any means—electronic, mechanical, photocopying, recording, or otherwise—without the prior written permission of Lerner Publishing Group, Inc., except for the inclusion of brief quotations in an acknowledged review.

Lerner Publications Company
A division of Lerner Publishing Group, Inc.
241 First Avenue North
Minneapolis, MN 55401 USA

For reading levels and more information, look up this title at www.lernerbooks.com.

The images in this book are used with the permission of: National Park Service, p. 30; Library of Congress (LC-DIG-pga-02091), p. 31.

Main body text set in Rotis Serif Std 55 Regular 15/24.
Typeface provided by Adobe Systems.

Library of Congress Cataloging-in-Publication Data

Names: Marsico, Katie, 1980– author. | Belmonte, David, illustrator.
Title: John Cook's Civil War story / by Katie Marsico ; illustrated by David
    Belmonte.
Description: Minneapolis : Lerner Publications, 2018. | Series: Narrative nonfiction:
    kids in war | Audience: Age: 7-10 | Audience: Grade: K to grade 3.
Identifiers: LCCN 2017004836 (print) | LCCN 2017025663 (ebook) |
    ISBN 9781512497823 (eb pdf) | ISBN 9781512456806 (lb : alk. paper)
Subjects: LCSH: Cook, John, 1847-1915—Juvenile literature. | United States—
    History—Civil War, 1861-1865—Participation, Juvenile—Juvenile literature. |
    United States—History—Civil War, 1861-1865—Biography—Juvenile literature. |
    Child soldiers—United States—Biography—Juvenile literature. | Antietam,
    Battle of, Md., 1862—Juvenile literature. | Medal of Honor—Biography—
    Juvenile literature.
Classification: LCC E540.C47 (print) | LCC E540.C47 M4739 2018 (ebook) |
    DDC 973.7092 [B]—dc23

LC record available at https://lccn.loc.gov/2017004836

Manufactured in the United States of America
1-42949-26765-8/22/2017

FOREWORD

From 1861 to 1865, the Civil War divided the United States. Starting in 1860, eleven Southern states decided to break apart from the rest of the nation. They formed the Confederate States of America, or the Confederacy. The states that did not break away were called the Union. Fighting soon left both sides desperate for new soldiers. The Confederacy and the Union started to take younger recruits. Sometimes a boy as young as twelve or thirteen was able to join.

To avoid defeat, Union forces had to prevent the Confederate army from pushing north. So Union troops attacked Confederate soldiers near Sharpsburg, Maryland, in what would later be called the Battle of Antietam.

SEPTEMBER 17, 1862, SHARPSBURG, MARYLAND

Thick, gray clouds hung over the Maryland countryside. The smell of burning gunpowder made John Cook's eyes water. He rubbed them as he coughed. Crouching down, he crawled through the battle.

John had joined the Union troops as a bugler and had even taken on the role of a messenger for some battles. But this day was different. John had little choice but to fight alongside his unit in what would be the bloodiest day of fighting during the Civil War.

Many of the men who usually
operated the cannons for his unit were
either wounded or dead. They lay on
the grass around John as Confederate
cannonballs roared overhead. The few
men who hadn't fallen were struggling
to carry on.

"Keep fighting, boys!" yelled a Union officer. John took a quick breath and prepared to join the battle. Though he was only fifteen, he was determined to do whatever it took to fight the Confederates.

THE EARLY HOURS OF ANTIETAM

John struggled to make his way through the thick smoke. All around him, soldiers prepared for battle. When he joined the Union army as a bugler just before he turned fourteen, John couldn't have imagined the chaos of war. John's bugle playing sent messages to the troops. He had brought calm and order. But it would take far more than bugle calls to help fight the Battle of Antietam.

As dawn broke on September 17,
the Union troops began their attack,
and soon fighting tore apart the woods
and cornfields near Antietam Creek.
John's unit prepared their cannons, but
a wave of Confederate bullets hit them.
Men and horses fell to the ground.
John ducked, knowing that another
round of fire could be coming at any
moment.

"You there! Cook!" barked General John Gibbon, one of John's commanding officers. "Captain Campbell's been shot. Move him away from the action!" John nodded and slung Campbell's arm over his shoulder. He began pulling the captain away from the front lines.

"Cook," Campbell mumbled as John dragged him along. "There's no time to lose, so listen. You need to head back there. A lot of our men went down . . . I'd guess we lost one or two dozen. Many of them were manning the cannons, Cook. We need your help."

Campbell paused. The battle was still raging, but they had made their way to a safe distance away from the front lines. John lowered the captain to the ground as gently as he could.

"Cook, try to find Lieutenant James Stewart." Campbell was holding his shoulder. A dark, red pool was spreading across his jacket and down his sleeve. "Tell Stewart he's in charge of whatever cannons and men we have left."

"Yes, sir," John replied. As he turned to face the front lines, his heart pounded in his chest.

BACK TO THE HEAT OF BATTLE

Once John spotted his unit through the haze of battle, he knew Campbell had been right. Only a handful of men were still fighting. Those that hadn't been injured or killed struggled to control their weapons. A few of the cannons were aimed too high. Explosions briefly lit up the sky, but the cannon fire wasn't slowing the Confederates down. John knew his unit was in trouble.

John had never loaded or fired
a cannon, but he had seen what
happened to the men who did it wrong.
They were often burned, and some lost
their arms and legs. Others even died.

As John rushed back to his unit, he heard Lieutenant Stewart shouting at the men. A few anxious soldiers looked up at him.

"What are you doing," the lieutenant barked at one of them. "Are you crazy? You must be, if you'd try to load a cannon like that! You'll blow us all to bits!" The man tried to answer Stewart, but John couldn't tell what he said. His words were drowned out by the crackle of gunfire. The endless, terrible noise covered the battlefield like a blanket. It rang in John's ears until he noticed the lieutenant's lips moving. Stewart was staring in John's direction.

THE STRUGGLE TO SAVE THE UNIT

"Well, soldier?" Stewart's voice snapped John back to attention. "Why are you just standing there? Can't you see those Confederates getting closer?" Before John could respond, a Confederate cannon belched out smoke and shook the ground.

"We need to reposition our guns," Stewart muttered. "Fast." Stewart turned his horse and prepared to charge into the thick haze that surrounded them.

"Sir, Captain Campbell ordered that you take command of our unit," John shouted. "He asked me to find you and tell you, sir." The lieutenant glanced over his shoulder. He gave John a long, hard look filled with both pity and impatience.

"We need to move forward if we are ever going to stop the Confederates," Stewart replied. With that, the lieutenant set off to join the cannons leading the battle. John rubbed his forehead as he tried to think clearly. Of course, Stewart was right. They needed to push the Confederates back. Wherever he looked, he saw proof of his enemies' success. But then he saw something else too.

As John glanced at a fallen soldier, he spied a worn leather pouch the man had been carrying. John lifted it and gently opened the flap. The pouch held cannon ammunition. If John was careful, he could load the ammunition into a cannon and begin firing at the enemy. If he was lucky, he could help stop the Confederate soldiers coming toward his unit.

TURNING A CANNON ON THE CONFEDERATES

John crept past bodies and through dark clouds of gun smoke. At last, he reached an open cannon. He fumbled to open the ammunition pouch. John had watched the men in his unit fire cannons before. But had he watched closely enough? Just one misstep and he might meet the same deadly fate as many of the soldiers around him.

"Right behind you, boy," boomed General Gibbon's familiar voice. The general leaped off his horse and stood by the cannon next to John. Normally a group of men handled the guns. Sometimes as many as seven. But John and the general knew they would have to make it work with just the two of them. Another round of explosions echoed nearby. "Are you ready, Cook?" Gibbon shouted over the noise.

"Yes, sir." John took a deep breath. "I found some ammunition that belonged to one of the other men."

"Good work," said Gibbon. "But we need to get it in the cannon before it'll do us any good." Through the noise and smoke, the general yelled orders to John as they loaded the cannon. John tried to focus but was distracted by an especially loud explosion. He looked up and saw a line of Confederate troops nearly upon them.

"They're only about fifteen feet from us now," said Gibbon, as if he could read John's thoughts. "Maybe even less than that. So, Cook, give the trigger string a pull . . . and drive the enemy back."

"Yes, sir," John said. He tugged on the string. When the cannon fired, it shook violently. John stumbled backward from the force of the explosion. He shielded his eyes against the chunks of dirt and grass that whipped in all directions around him.

John searched for the Confederates who had been swarming toward them moments before. When he didn't see them, he spun around and scanned the horizon. Instead of glimpsing the Confederates' gray uniforms, he spotted the faint blue outlines of other Union soldiers.

"Backup is here," hollered Gibbon. "Now those Confederates will *really* hear some cannon fire!" The general shook John's hand. "Of course, you gave them a taste of that yourself, didn't you, Cook?"

AFTERWORD

During the Battle of Antietam, almost twenty-three thousand men were wounded, went missing, or were killed. Some historians say neither side won because each suffered such heavy losses. Still, Union troops accomplished an important goal of pushing the Confederate forces out of Maryland.

After the Battle of Antietam, John continued serving with the Union army. Decades later, John's courage was not forgotten. In 1894, the US military awarded him the Medal of Honor for his efforts in Maryland.

TIMELINE

August 16, 1847 John Cook is born in Hamilton County, Ohio.

December 20, 1860 South Carolina breaks away from the Union. Ten other Southern states will eventually follow.

April 12, 1861 In South Carolina, the first official military conflict erupts between Union and Confederate forces.

June 7, 1861 John enlists with the Union army. He serves as a bugler.

September 17, 1862 The Battle of Antietam occurs near Antietam Creek in Sharpsburg, Maryland. John helps protect his unit during the battle.

July 1–3, 1863 John participates in the Battle of
Gettysburg in Pennsylvania.

April 9, 1865
Confederate general
Robert E. Lee
surrenders to Union
forces in Virginia,
ending the war.

June 30, 1894 The US military awards Cook the
Medal of Honor for his efforts at the Battle
of Antietam.

August 3, 1915 Cook dies. Later, his body is
buried in Arlington National Cemetery
in Virginia.

LEARN MORE ABOUT JOHN COOK

BOOKS

Bearce, Stephanie. *The Civil War.* Waco, TX: Prufrock, 2015. Read all about the top secret spies, hidden facts, and exciting secret missions of the Civil War.

Figley, Marty Rhodes. *President Lincoln, Willie Kettles, and the Telegraph Machine.* Minneapolis: Millbrook Press, 2011. Find out how the telegraph ended the US Civil War and learn about the men behind the true story.

Ratliff, Thomas. *You Wouldn't Want to Be a Civil War Soldier! A War You'd Rather Not Fight.* New York: Franklin Watts, 2013. Explore a timeline of major events that shaped the war, as well as how they would have affected your life if you were around during the battles.

WEBSITES

BrainPOP—Civil War
https://www.brainpop.com/socialstudies/ushistory/civilwar/
Check out movies, maps, and a variety of activities involving the Civil War.

Civil War Saga—Child Soldiers in the Civil War
http://civilwarsaga.com/child-soldiers-in-the-civil-war/
Visit this site to read more about John Cook and other young soldiers who fought during the Civil War.

Ducksters—Battle of Antietam
http://www.ducksters.com/history/civil_war/battle_of_antietam.php
Find fast facts and take a ten-question quiz about the Battle of Antietam.